# Her  Our Paris?

# Hemingway's Paris:

# Our Paris?

## H.R. Stoneback

2010
New Street Communications, LLC
Wickford, RI

newstreetcommunications.com

Copyright 1990 and 2010 by H.R. Stoneback.

All rights reserved under International and Pan-American Copyright Conventions. Except for brief quotations for review purposes, no part of this book may be reproduced in any form without the permission of New Street Communications, LLC.

Published by New Street Communications, LLC
Wickford, Rhode Island
newstreetcommunications.com

Cover art *Notre Dame de Paris 2* by Albert Lebourg (1849-1928), courtesy of private collection.

# Publisher's Note

Written during the late 1980s and originally published as a small limited edition chapbook in 1990, H.R. Stoneback's *Hemingway's Paris: Our Paris?* is a masterpiece of both appreciation and analysis by a scholar whose knowledge and love of Paris is as deep, profound and genuine as his knowledge and love of Hemingway. We at New Street are proud to make this important work available to a new generation of readers.

H.R. Stoneback is Distinguished Professor of English at the State University of New York, New Paltz. Stoneback has received numerous awards and honors for criticism, poetry and teaching. He has served as visiting professor at the University of Paris, Fulbright Professor at Peking University and director of the American Center for Students and Artists in Paris. A leading scholar of international reputation on Ernest Hemingway, Stoneback is also a widely published literary critic, poet and author or editor of more than 20 volumes of criticism and poetry. His recent books include *Reading Hemingway's "The Sun Also Rises"* (Kent State University Press, 2007) and *Hurricane Hymn and Other Poems* (Codhill Press, 2009). Stoneback is a former member of the Board of Directors of the Hemingway Society.

# I

> *"If you are lucky enough to have lived in Paris as a young man, then wherever you go for the rest of your life, it stays with you, for Paris is a moveable feast."* – Hemingway, *A Moveable Feast*

Every year thousands of Americans make the pilgrimage to search for Hemingway's Paris – is it still there? Is Papa's "moveable feast" still moving? Recently, when I posed these questions to a friend, a French writer and farmer in Provence who left Paris for good in the wake of the 1968 rebellion, he said: "Paris? C'est termineé." Then he thought a moment and added: "Hemingway? C'est termineé." Although I know what he meant, given his post-modern, neo-agrarian viewpoint, I cannot believe that either assertion is true. Yet his remarks compelled me to make an examination of conscience. I had assumed for some years that I knew exactly what Hemingway's Paris was, but I had never examined the matter, just as I had not questioned my Paris – a place I had loved naturally and completely from the first day I set foot in it. I discovered that not only was I incapable of immediately articulating my Paris, of giving an exact constatation, but I was not at all sure what it had to do with Hemingway's Paris. Thus I decided that if I could define these subtle relationships I might be able to speak for some of my contemporaries – those of us who have known Paris in the 60s, 70s, and 80s – and determine if our Paris had anything to do with Hemingway's Paris. For surely, it was important since neither Hemingway nor Paris was over, finished, terminated: they would always be there when you needed them.

# II

*"This is a good town. Why don't you start living your life in Paris?"* – Jake Barnes in *The Sun Also Rises*

All Americans come to Paris first as tourists, now that we do not go anymore as soldiers redeeming the ancient amity. Some stay on, some return again and again, some adopt Paris as aesthetic home, spiritual home, as the only city on earth where a fully civilized life is possible. Those who stay long enough come to understand what Thomas Jefferson meant when he said that every man has two countries, his own and Paris, and what Gertrude Stein felt when she said: "America is my country and Paris is my home town." But when we arrive for the first time, even if we haven't read much Hemingway, ineluctably we see Paris through his eyes: the light, the night, the life of the streets, the style and the stillness, and, above all, the cafés. It only takes a college course or two to set the stage – and few who make it through high school to a freshman year of college fail to read *The Sun Also Rises* in one course or another. Throw in a reading of *A*

*Moveable Feast*, add a viewing of a Hemingway film or two, and the initiate is prepared for apprenticeship in Hemingway's Paris. *The Sun Also Rises* serves to set the ceremony in motion: drinks at the famous cafés mentioned in the novel, the Closerie des Lilas, Dôme, Rotonde, Select and all the others, followed by walks in Jake's footsteps on the rue de la Montagne Sainte Genevieve, the Boulevards Montparnasse and St. Michel, around the Ile Saint Louis and up the rue du Cardinal Lemoine to the Place Contrescarpe and on over to the rue Saint-Jacques. The apprentice will probably see the river, the barges, and Notre Dame in the night sky, through Jake's eyes. And, with luck and a little more reading, the tourist apprentice may deepen the Hemingway ritual through *A Moveable Feast*, seeing the rue Mouffetard, "that wonderful narrow crowded market street"; "the ancient church of St.-Etienne-du-Mont and the windswept Place du Pantheon"; the "fresh-washed gravel paths" of the Luxembourg Gardens and the "sculpture" of the bare trees in winter; the river, the fishermen, the bookstalls on the quais; and, with the right hotel room in the right location, "all the roofs and the chimneys of the high hill of the quarter." Or maybe it will be mainly the cafés and the brasseries mentioned in the book, always the drinking and with it the failure to recognize that *A Moveable Feast* is a book about love and discipline, about writing, about a Paris that is "the town best organized for a writer to write in that there is."

No, the Hemingway tourist who conducts his Parisian novitiate primarily in the cafés is not likely to find Hemingway's Paris, for "Paris [is] a very old city .... and nothing [is] simple there." And nothing is simple in Hemingway. Few such apprentices are likely to be aware of Hemingway's lifelong contempt for café trash, for the "weird lot" which he scorned as early as 1922 when he wrote an article, "American Bohemians in Paris," which describes "the scum of Greenwich Village" who have been "skimmed off and deposited in large ladlesful on that section of Paris adjacent to the Café Rotonde .... a strange-acting and strange-looking breed." Perhaps the saddest thing is that some Hemingway tourists may never come to see that they are engaged in an action contrary to the spirit of Hemingway's vision, that they are doing precisely what he tells them they must not do; many of them will never understand why Jake Barnes avoids "the sad tables of the Rotonde," or what Hemingway meant when he said the novel is a tract against "promiscuity." Once, at the Rotonde, in a season when they were serving a particularly good salade Bretonne, I sat at my favorite side table where the view of Rodin's Balzac in the winter drizzle is particularly fine. A young Hemingway enthusiast, a college sophomore spending his winter break in Paris, spoke to me, told me that he was determined to consume every kind of drink mentioned in *The Sun Also Rises*, and to do it in every café mentioned in the novel. He only had a week to do it in, and he was very determined. I have wondered about his fate, wondered if he found the Hemingway's Paris that he was looking for. I doubt it, but then he was a very pleasant, accurate young man, with great curiosity, and it may be that, eventually, after he was through with the drinks and the cafés, he did find Hemingway's Paris. But I knew that he would not find it that week, not in his list of cafés and drinks.

# III

*"There is only one place to live forever, Paris."* – Ingrid Bergman to Hemingway in A.E. Hotchner, *Papa Hemingway*

When I first went to Paris to *live*, I was resolved to avoid what I thought of then as Hemingway's superficial Paris, since I was firm in my will to live quietly and deeply into the real Paris, to enter truly into the life of France, and this resolve would have no truck with shallow American expatriate notions. Early in that first year of residence in Paris I had my first conversation with James Jones, a central figure in yet another generation of American expatriate writers in France:

> "So what are you kid? Another young American novelist looking for Hemingway's ghost?" His eyebrows furrowed down and deeply inward.
> "No," I said. "I'm more interested in Baudelaire and St.-John Perse."

"Sure." Jones frowned. "So you're not hot on Papa's trail?"

"Not at all." He couldn't believe that I really wasn't.

"You come here to write or to drink at all of Hemingway's old hangouts?"

"Are you buying?" I laughed.

Jones's scowl turned darker as he went on to talk about Hemingway's Paris, a Paris which didn't exist, he insisted; but there was something he wasn't saying, some deep sense of unredeemed debt, some tangled sense of resentment toward Hemingway that I sensed between the lines, as if Hemingway had somehow led Jones to an illusory Paris all those years ago, as if Hemingway was guilty of some kind of personal betrayal of Jones. (Later, when I read *The Merry Month of May*, I concluded that although Jones, in a way, knew and loved one Paris, it was his Paris that didn't exist, and Hemingway's that always would.)

When, talking with James Jones and others that year, I confessed my indifference to Hemingway, and professed my far greater interest in French writers, I was probably telling a truth that I deeply felt at the time. After all, I had not read Hemingway for many years and by the sheer force of cultural complicity, at least, I shared in the ill-informed condescension toward Hemingway that had become fashionable in the 1960s. I had liked Hemingway's stuff when I was a kid, but, as I was saying in those days, I had graduated to Faulkner a long time ago. In fact, if I was interested in the trail of any American writer in Paris, it was Faulkner's spoor I would follow down the rue Servandoni to St. Sulpice, and back again to the Luxembourg Gardens, wondering why he had stayed in Paris only a few months though he had so obviously loved it. (But I knew about Mississippi and the South, how it was all different from Hemingway's Midwest, so I understood why Faulkner went home and Hemingway never did.) That year, I was teaching a seminar in Faulkner at the University of Paris. It would not have occurred to me to offer a seminar in Hemingway, and nobody suggested it. Even there, everyone seemed to think Hemingway was passé.

So I went my way, in a disciplined disregard of Hemingway's Paris. Sometimes it came too close, as when I ran into American writers and writerly tourists at cafés and parties, or at that splendid bookstore, Shakespeare and Company, where everyone had to stop in now and then because George Whitman ran (still runs) a fine well-stocked place that everyone needed sometime. There, at one evening reading, I heard a young poet from the West Coast read – she had a flat inflectionless voice and glazed eyes – a poem about a fly on a priest's nose and then another that alluded to Hemingway's "phony machismo" and "woman-hating," a tedious arhythmic exercise in atrabilious misperception; luckily, she was interrupted by another young poet who averred in a kind of rambling prose-poem that he had seen, in a vision that very afternoon, Baudelaire talking with

Hemingway on the North Tower of Notre Dame; he didn't catch what they said, for they were talking in street French. When the reading was over, a South American poet with his shirt open to his navel, a bottle of Scotch and a hunting knife tucked in his belt, informed me that the mythical Paris of the 1920s was "phony," that Hemingway was not so "tough," that Fitzgerald couldn't handle his liquor, and that this Paris, *his* Paris, the "kingdom of Soixante-huit" was the real thing. I said nothing. He took my silence for assent, and offered me a joint and a drink from the Scotch bottle in his belt. I declined, and went outside, went back into France, trying to escape the myth, all the silly myths of Hemingway. Another day at Shakespeare's, I encountered a professor and a graduate student who were comparing notes and detailed maps tracing all of Hemingway's peregrinations in Paris. They were very concerned with accuracy. They asked me a question. I told them I knew nothing about it, nothing at all. But, in the end, no matter what you did, you could not escape Hemingway's Paris.

    For a while, I thought that I could. I would spend the day at my office at the American Center for Students and Artists, planning a revival of *The Montparnasse Review*, and then, after work, walk down the Boulevard Raspail to meet a friend at the Dôme and never once think of Hemingway. We would eat at Lipps, go up on the hill afterwards, do the clubs, or go to a bal musette where neighborhood locals still danced to an ancient accordion player, and never once think of Hemingway. We would get up early and on a fine clean bright morning walk through the Luxembourg and under the blooming *marroniers* and have coffee and brioche on the rue Soufflot and not think of Hemingway. We could walk around Ile Saint Louis at night, study the *arcs-boutant* of the Cathedral from the bridges, or buy books at noon in the stalls along the river and read in the sun by the water in the magical Vert-Galant and Hemingway's shadow was not there. Or so we thought.

Not long after I moved to the rue Saint-Jacques, I picked up a copy of *The Sun Also Rises* at Shakespeare and Company. I had not read it since the early 1960s when I was living in New Orleans, when I had not yet been to Paris, but I was serving my apprenticeship in the French Quarter, where many of us reenacted our Louisiana version of fiesta, of *The Sun Also Rises* as we understood it then. (Decades later, just recently, I would finally come to understand how New Orleans and the then-enchanted French Quarter had prepared my love for Paris.) So I reread the novel, sitting in my window looking out across the rue Saint-Jacques to Val-de-Grâce. Then it happened: Hemingway's Paris came alive for me.

It started with the recognition that part of what I felt about living in the exact place where I did had something to do with Hemingway's evocation of the rue Saint-Jacques and Val-de-Grâce in the novel. Then I realized that what I had always felt about walking and riding on the Boulevard Raspail, the street that I went to work on every day, had been implanted in me by

Hemingway years before. I felt that parts of Raspail were dead and dull and ugly, and I hated driving on it, though walking certain parts was all right. Then, for the first time in all those years, I read Jake's meditation about the "dead places" and I understood why I felt as I did:

> *There are other streets in Paris as ugly as the Boulevard Raspail. It is a street I do not mind walking down at all. But I cannot stand to ride along it. Perhaps I had read something about it once.*

And when I walked home late down the dark silent Boulevard Montparnasse, past the Closerie and Marshall Ney, it was the same thing, the ur-Paris eidolon and echo given to me unacknowledged by the novel years before that finally achieved consciousness:

> *The Boulevard Montparnasse was deserted .... they were stacking the tables outside the Closerie des Lilas. I passed Ney's statue standing among the new-leaved chestnut trees in the arc-light .... He looked very fine, Marshall Ney in his top-boots, gesturing with his sword among the green new horse-chestnut leaves.*

Yes, I had passed Marshall Ney a hundred times and felt the same thing, noticed the same details, without realizing that both Ney *and* Hemingway had been gesturing at me. So I learned that part of the way I felt about many things in Paris, about crossing bridges, about certain streets and cafés, about the pervasive numinous feeling of place, had come to me from Hemingway. Then I studied it and tried to understand how it worked, how a casual reading of a novel more than a decade earlier could so deeply imprint on my imagination the spirit of place, the details and the emotion of Hemingway's Paris. Some of it had to do with style, with the clean aesthetic space and authority that surrounds each of Hemingway's words when he is at his best. But there was something else.

  I learned what it was one day at my regular corner café. I had been brooding the topography and cartography of *The Sun Also Rises*, of Jake's itineraries; I was particularly puzzled by Hemingway's description of the rue Saint-Jacques – there, in my winding medieval neighborhood – as "the rigid north and south of the Rue Saint-Jacques." Why would the writer who always told it as it was (or so we were taught) change the facts? Why would the ostensible master of precision so clearly distort the actual conformation of a street which he knew well? I raised this question in conversation at the café with a lifelong denizen of the Saint-Jacques *quartier*. Yes, he knew about Hemingway; no, he had not read his *romans*. So I read to him the "rigid north and south" passage, and he pondered the matter in silence over his calvados. He looked at the passage in question, asked about the action and the other settings of the novel but said nothing about it that day.

The next day he sat with me at the café and after some talk of the weather he asked: "Do you know of Saint-Jacques de Compostelle?" No, I said, what was that? "Do you know, then, Santiago de Compostela?" Yes, I had heard of it – it was a place in Spain. "More than a place, my friend. Come, walk with me." We walked a few blocks along the rue Saint-Jacques. He said I was right, the street is not rigid – it is medieval, it bends. The boulevards, the positivist creations of the 19$^{th}$ century, are rigid. He asked me if I knew that Val-de-Grâce was a famous church, monastery *and* a hospital for wounded soldiers. Yes, I knew that. (And I understood why Jake, a wounded soldier, had noted it during his walk.) He pointed out the entrance to the famous Convent of the Carmelites and spoke of the associations with St. Theresa of Avila. (Later, much later, I would find Hemingway's commentary on St. Theresa.) He identified the *Institut Des Sourds-Muets*, the National Institute of the Deaf and Dumb, and made a joke about how it stood in the place where, for many centuries, there had been an important hospice for the pilgrims to Santiago de Compostela. He was not very religious, he said, but he was much in love with history. He pointed out the church of Saint-Jacques-du-Haut-Pas, another pilgrim church. In rapid succession he showed me the site of the house where Jean de Meung finished the *Roman de la Rose*, the site of the Saint-Jacques gate in the old city wall, and the College of Saint Barbara where St. Ignace de Loyola had been a student. (Later, I would learn that before he gave his Nobel Prize Medal to the Shrine of the Virgin of Cobre, Hemingway had considered giving it to Saint Barbara, patron saint of artillerymen and those in danger of sudden death; and I would see the plaque in the street of that other pilgrimage town, Pamplona, marking the spot where, during the siege of Pamplona, Loyola had been badly wounded – like Hemingway, in the legs, by artillery – the "wound that made him think," as Hemingway described Loyola's wound which turned him from soldier to saint.) We had a drink at a café on the rue Soufflot and my friend showed me the site of yet another celebrated hospice for the pilgrims of Saint-Jacques, a resting place on the long way south to Bayonne, Roncevaux, Pamplona and on out to Santiago de Compostela. I did not fully understand it then but I had just been given a tour of touchstones in Hemingway's life and work, a key that would open the door to the mysterious resonances of Hemingway's Paris, and of the other numinous places in his world such as Santiago which he thought "the loveliest town in Spain," where he spent three summers "working on [his] education."

As we walked back toward Val-de-Grâce, my neighbor-guide said something like this: So, you see, we are walking the ancient route of millions of pilgrims, Saint-Jacques – Santiago – is a place and the way that takes you there is a part of the place. This famous rue Saint-Jacques is a sign we can no longer interpret of the vast, secret ceremony of our civilization, now lost, in this sad twentieth century. The pilgrimage of Saint-Jacques is – how do you say? – a *constatation emblematique* of not only the history, but the art, the beauty, the feeling, the belief – the very spirit of Western Civilization (he spoke this in upper case). It is, then, "rigid north and south" only in the strict light of history, in the suffering and joy, the expiation and renewal of the great *pèlerinage*. Although I have not read him much, it seems your Monsieur Hemingway knew more history and was perhaps more *Catholique* than most Americans. *Après tout*, he was concerned with much more than the naturalistic surface of things. Yes, I said, it did seem that way.

    And so, I could no longer walk the streets of Hemingway's Paris in a carefree and casual fashion, for there were new things to think about as I followed Jake's footsteps (even his *name* marks him as a pilgrim). I noted, on down the rue Saint-Jacques, a café called Le Compostelle which I had not truly seen before. Sometimes, late at night, Jake's and Hemingway's footsteps seemed to echo under my window and I would look out and see only the great dome of Val-de-Grâce in the moonlight and grieve for all the wounded soldiers and pilgrims long gone down the legendary pilgrim highway. *The Sun Also Rises* came to seem the exact analogue to the great medieval pilgrim's guide and original best-selling travel book, the *Liber Sancti Jacobi*, which told the pilgrims how to conduct themselves as they traveled through France and across the Pyrenees into Spain. My friend's lesson in topography and history led to an unfolding of the numinous sense, the anagogical level of Hemingway's work which has been unceasing, which has brought me, through pilgrimages great and small, back to Hemingway, the real Hemingway of the true moveable feast (as the Church calendar expresses the matter). It *is* a pilgrim's feast, with Paris holding the center, and there is never any end to it.

# IV

*"The Quarter without Ernest Hemingway has lost something – he helped us to see it through his own eyes."* – Sisley Huddleston, Back to Montparnasse

If Hemingway has helped us all to see Paris through his own eyes, why have so many of us seen so little of what he put into his work, of the symbolic landscapes which inform the novels and the stories? One reason, I suppose, has been our insufficient grasp of his principles of understatement, his strategy of allusion, and what he called his "theory of omission" whereby what the writer knowingly omits or merely hints at is as important as what is put in, and what is between the lines makes the reader feel more than is understood. This complex matter may better be left to exercises in literary criticism in academic journals, but if, as in Hemingway's famous metaphor evoking the nature of good writing, "the dignity of movement of an ice-berg is due to only one-eighth of it being above water," then the tips of the "ice-bergs" which show in much of his work are the spires and towers of the cathedrals and churches which compose the skylines in his narratives. Hemingway's world is a resacralized landscape and few writers have responded as deeply as he did to the *deus loci*, the spirit of place, residing in each place he evoked. He is one of our great poets of place, at once a very accurate and rapt cartographer and bard of the *deus loci*. And yet most of us, at one time or another, slumber in thralldom to the silly myth of the Lost Generation, foolish and firm in our windy asseverations that Hemingway's world is a world of drunken expatriates aimlessly drifting from Paris to Spain and back again with no point, no direction, stoically enduring the night and *nada* in a world where all values are lost, all gods dead. It would seem almost impossible to escape this view of Hemingway since it has been sold in our classrooms for half a century, promulgated in magazines and on television screens by almost everyone who talks about Hemingway. And they all do; *everyone* seems to think he or she knows all about Hemingway – people who wouldn't dream of opening their mouths about Faulkner or Joyce, say, will go on and on about Hemingway even if they haven't read his work. The relentless cultural bombardment, the incessant advertisements for the Lost Generation, seem to have impaired the capacity of readers to see anything but the false inverted image of Hemingway and his work that is both so cherished, so despised. But the Lost Generation is a product that Hemingway never sold, and those who knew never bought it.

  One of those who never bought it was Allen Tate, poet-critic-novelist and friend of Hemingway, especially in Paris in the late 1920s. I vividly remember the night in 1967 when Tate told me that Hemingway was "very Catholic" when he knew him in Paris in 1929, that they had gone to Mass and to the bicycle races together. When I encouraged Tate to tell more about Paris in those golden days he spoke of how Hemingway took "keen pleasure" in showing him the Paris that he loved: "He really did love it as a *place* with a kind of magic, you know. And as a center of civilization."

Pursuing the notion of what Hemingway's Paris was to others, and looking back over my notes and journals and letters from the past two decades, I also find this: Mary Hemingway telling me about the great delight that Ernest took in showing her "his true Paris" in the 1940s and 50s, in walking with her the streets of "the city that he loved best in all the world." It was, she said, a rare pleasure to see it through his eyes. And what she saw had nothing to do with any superficial Lost Generation notions. When I asked her about the making of *A Moveable Feast* she was understandably reluctant to talk about the later details of the posthumous publication of that book, but she did recall that when his spirits were low in the late 1950s he would cheer himself up by working on the book, reliving and remaking Paris in "memory and art."

Ten years ago, on a long ride through the Hudson Valley countryside, Malcolm Cowley and I talked for hours about the 1920s, about Paris, about Hemingway. Much of what he said that day — about Hemingway's manner of absolutely filling and focusing any room he entered, about his vitality and "enormous quiet charm," his "essential mystery," about how Hemingway was "the great star of Paris" and "the most charming person I ever met but also the most difficult" – Cowley had said in print. But it was one thing to read such observations, quite another to hear them delivered with poignant enduring conviction by a man just past his 80th birthday looking back over the better part of a century. When we reached his home in Sherman, Connecticut, we were still talking about Hemingway and Paris; there was one thing he said which I have not found in any of his books or essays, which I wrote down when he left the room: "It was as if all Paris belonged to him, and what he most wanted was to present it to you, to make an offering of it with great humility and devotion, to give Paris to you as a precious and personal gift." I could not tell whether this was Cowley's exact personal sense of the man or a distillation of the essence of Hemingway's work – it was probably compounded of both – but I felt the immediate rightness of Cowley's words. The gift of Paris was given by Hemingway in the same manner that Santiago, the old fisherman, would give the great gift of the Gulf Stream. (And now, as I write this sentence, I hear on the radio the news of Cowley's death, at 90, and I publicly grieve, and thank Malcolm Cowley for *his* gifts – of Paris, of Hemingway, of so many things – to all of us.)

In the early 1980s I was living one fall and winter in a lonely chateau in the Provençal countryside, and when the

Mistral blew (and when it didn't) I was sometimes homesick for Paris. I was working on a volume of poetry, on a Hemingway essay or two, and I was studying the poetry of St.-John Perse. I was fascinated by certain connections between Perse and Hemingway: they had in common long periods of expatriation or exile from their native countries, friendships with Archibald MacLeish and Allen Tate, and apparently they had met a few times in the 1920s. But I was more interested in the quality of "vital reverence," as Perse calls it, that both writers possessed, and in the way that Perse's belief that "poetic creation has no other object than the liberating of joy .... the most sacred of pleasures" could be applied to the fundamental thrust of Hemingway's work. (*The Sun Also Rises* and *A Moveable Feast*, for example, are not *about* "joy," but they "liberate" joy, exhale a "vital reverence.")

One afternoon, over a fine lunch at "Les Vigneaux," St.-John Perse's (i.e., Alexis Leger's) home on the Mediterranean at Presqu'Ile de Giens, one of the loveliest spots on the Côte d'Azur, I asked Dorothy Leger about Hemingway and her husband. She thought that he had mentioned Hemingway a time or two, that they had met in Paris in the 20s. We spoke about Paris, then, and Madame Leger said, no, she did not think her husband's Paris had much to do with Hemingway's Paris. (I knew what she meant: after all, her husband, aside from the sideline Nobel Prize winning vocation of poet, had a distinguished career as a diplomat until he fled to the U.S. from the Nazis in 1940.)

After lunch, we admired the sea view from the rooftop terrace, walked the ancient custom officer's path along the rim of the cliff, and retired to Perse's study. There, among the mementoes and echoes of Paul Claudel, Joseph Conrad, T.S. Eliot and Paul Valéry, of Dag Hammarskjöld, the John F. Kennedys, Igor Stravinsky and all the others, Madame Leger took up the thread of our lunchtime conversation:

"I suppose all Americans have to get their Paris, their France, filtered through Franklin, Jefferson, Cooper, James and yes, maybe now, in these times, through Hemingway before all others."

"Where else will they get it," I said, "given the death of history? They don't read the old writers anymore."

"You must be right – what do I know about it?" She smiled and I saw that she knew a good deal about it. "But why did Hemingway have all that false romanticism about being poor in Paris – what was it? Killing pigeons in the Luxembourg Gardens for supper, taking them home in the baby's carriage? Surely he never did that?"

"I doubt it," I said.

"Didn't he really prefer the Crillon and the Ritz to Montparnasse and the Place Contrescarpe?"

"I reckon so," I said. "But he didn't really tell that story."

"No, not at all."

"Maybe if he had lived longer," I said, but I knew it was not true. "Maybe he would have written the sequel to *A Moveable Feast*: Part One – Young and Poor in Paris; Part Two – Old and Rich and Famous in Paris?"

"All that youth and poverty business, so jaded, so false," she said. "But then, Paris, of course, is kind of miraculous. Paris can make you believe anything."

"Yes," I said. "As writers go, Hemingway could make you believe anything when he was writing well. And as places go, Paris is a kind of miracle, it changes you. It changed him."

# V

*"All Paris belongs to me and I belong to this notebook and this pencil."* – Hemingway, *A Moveable Feast*

What, then, is the "miracle," the "feast"? Every reader who knows Paris can make his own list, her own inventory, of the outward and visible signs. I can make my list: the narrow, leaning streets, the slanting walls of the 16th century houses, the laughter drifting out of tall windows behind iron-grilled balconies exploding with flowers; the way the clouds work over the white bubbles of Sacré-Coeur and if the angle and distance and light are right the way the pinnacles look like Byzantine rockets launched toward infinity with the white exhaust of the domes flowing back to the earth beneath, trembling under the unbelievable sound of the Savoyarde, the great twenty-ton bell; the lights along the river at night, on the water and on the arcing bridges, and how the smells of the darkness, the damp stone quais, the river and all Paris mingle; the sweptback curving rooflines in the morning light and the rooftops and chimneypots; the sculpted trees in winter and the sadness of the wintry economy of the pruned plane trees before the piles of limbs are taken away; the repose of the old men fishing on the quais and the angle of their long poles; the shadows and faces under the summer awnings, the different colors, lettering and varied umbrellafication of the café awnings – Flore, Deux-Magots, Dôme; the precise morning formation of the sidewalk tables and chairs and their midnight disposition, and the way the waiters' voices changed as the day moved; the swinging doors at Sank Roo Doe Noo, where you hadn't been in years but it was sometimes good to think that Harry's was still there and you could always go back; the openwork metal baker's handcarts on the streets in the early morning and the time you counted forty tall *baguettes* vertically stacked in one cart, upthrust like some fabulous fluted geological upheaval of the earth's mad crusted plentitude; but on the Ile Saint Louis they still use woven straw baker's carts so you cannot see the formation, the topography of the twisted crusts, just the tops of the *baguettes*. There, on the Ile, waking up in the morning, you hear the delivery trucks and the streetsweepers and the chatter of schoolchildren echoing in the narrow street under your window, and you open the window to the balcony and watch the kids with brightly colored school cases and packs on their backs, and hear the reverberant voice of the man from your *boulangerie* as he shouts something to the egg-lady down the street; as you drink your coffee in the window, you nod formally

and speak to the lady in the third-floor window across the
intimate street who is feeding the pigeons and at another window
you salute the cats lazing in the first sun catching the third-floor
windows and you are with all of these, living together in the
small things, and the day is bound together in a dear domesticity;
a dog barks somewhere and you hear the streetcry of the *vitrier*
and you watch him leaning into his slow musical walk with the
large wooden rack strapped on his back holding panes of glass
and you think of streetcries from childhood in another city long
ago, streetcries no longer heard, and this *vitrier* has a fine resonant
voice still echoing after he turns the corner, around there where
Baudelaire used to live; and, as always, you feel the river moving
around the Ile, you almost hear it, and sometimes it seems the
island is moving with the river, caught in the great Seine net,
meshed with all of France washing downstream as the bells from
Notre Dame drift across the water; and at night there is the
Brasserie, where even when he hasn't seen you for several years
the deep-voiced humorously raspy waiter remembers you and
your table and the *cassoulet* and *choucroute garni* and the large
mug of Mutzig you've ordered for decades; or, down the street at
the A.A.A.A. sign, where the amicable and ardent amateurs of
authentic andouillette gather, there is Monsieur Bourdeau, whose
servings are as generous as his spirit, who serves the best
andouillette and red beans in Paris, and where you feel at home
always, especially after Madame Bourdeau's miraculous stuffed
mussels in shallot butter; and then again, the bells, the profound

and solemn *bourdon* and *les cloches de la tour nord,* coming at you from the cathedral and the way it looks against the sky and how part of the way it looks against the night sky is how it feels to be inside in the afternoons when the light slants a certain way through the Rose Window and how the great organ sounds on a snowy winter afternoon at the recital before evening Mass. And all the rest of Paris, too, all the markets with the neat whitegreen stacks of leeks that you want to touch, with their fresh-washed root-hairs combed in the sun, the mysterious rows of artichokes and the great-knuckled fists of garlic, the kind reserved gentle cheerful market people, the fish markets and the schools of striped rainbowed *maquereaux* and lovely *loup* and flat round-diamond-shaped Plaice, the arrangement of the oysters of Locmariaquer and the Marennes of the Charente-Maritime, the mussels of the Loire-Atlantique, and next door in the window the platter of Coquilles Saint-Jacques, the pilgrim's shell, à la parisienne. In the Luxembourg Garden the clustered posture and the intensity of the earthbound gaze as the men measure off the *boules,* the fountained pool and the toy boats and the way it feels to walk on the bright gravel, how things sound when you take a chair in the sun and close your eyes hearing the kids shouting and the old men scuffing the gravel as they walk by talking softly and the cooing and kazooing of the pigeons and their thrumming heavy-winged takeoff and landing; you open your eyes and look up at the avenues of tall dark trees in the fading light and you walk past the sculpted queen with the flowing gown, her head cocked and chin lifted like a cat's when you scratch its chin, the large cross resting between her stone breasts and you love her as you have loved Houdon's *La Frileuse*; then the gardens are closed, the profoundest definition of *shut*, behind the great gold-tipped iron gates. All of it belongs to you, the distinct smell of every Metro station, the ornate gates and carved doors to all the secret courtyards, the clochards, the barges, the waiters and the priests, the poets and the dancers, all the museums, churches and cafés together with the view of Notre Dame from the andouillette and friterie stand tucked in the angled corner behind St. Julien-le-Pauvre. There used to be the welcome whooshing rush of heat from the fire-eater on a November night; and everything about how it was to finish singing at the club and then go out with the heirs and heiresses who were collecting writers and singers that season and how good it felt to leave them at dawn on the Champs, refusing a ride in the Rolls so you could flag your own honest taxi and ride into the light to your own neighborhood and have coffee and almond croissants at the little corner place across from the great dome of Val-de-Grâce. Then, too, there was how it felt to write in Paris. And to teach in Paris. There was also the stale precious look on the faces of the professors, French and American, Maoist and Deconstructionist alike, when they said they didn't really think there would be any possible interest in a literary evening devoted to the subject of American writers in Paris; the empty feeling of the sad classrooms and the dreary universities in the Maoist years after soixante-huit; and all the phony artists at the American Center. And, after singing all night at the Trois Mailletz and the private clubs, with your fingers hurting from the guitarstrings played too long and loud and liquidly, after onion soup at dawn in Les Halles before it was demolished and made into a stylish version of an American mall, there was the ethereal boys' choir and the sudden brass on Easter Sunday at the Cathedral, jammed in with all the saints and sinners, poets and drunkards, aristocrats and working-people; and how it felt at Christmas Eve Mass when, after moving down the aisle where the moiling undulant crowd wanted to take you, you stood still in the crush of all Paris and while the priest chanted you looked down at your feet and saw that you were standing on the spot marking the site of Claudel's conversion; and maybe that was a kind of literary event or at least it was somehow related to the way you felt when you found out, years afterwards, that the first room you stayed in on the rue des Sts. Pères for a week that very first time in Paris was the very same room where Ezra Pound had lived when he worked on *The Waste Land*, converting Eliot's manuscript to the litany we had always lived with and Hemingway had rewritten in prose from *In Our Time* to *The Old Man and the Sea*. And there were other literary evenings with French and American writers in lavish penthouses off *Etoile* and private receptions for artists in the town quarters of the Count and Countess, and many of the people at these affairs – in spite of their condescension to Hemingway as some kind of outré fisherman or gauche big-game hunter, bully, self-parodic monosyllabic mutterer – many were really trying to relive Hemingway's Paris, trying too hard and doing it with infinitely less style, grace, intelligence, and discipline. For all their patronizing talk of a Hemingway they would never know or understand, for all their talk about their own writing and painting, none of them would ever produce anything to outlast the next sunrise. Thus it was always very lucky to be able to go back to the other Paris, the real Paris of neighborhoods and working people, children and old people, the Paris of a thousand daily acts of kindness and civility and community, the Paris where an ancient true joy was liberated every day, the Paris where you could try to write certain things but you could not write anything about Paris for Hemingway had done it, and Hemingway's Paris was – *is* – our Paris. Still, you could try, because you had to when you were no longer living in Paris, and maybe you could make it new.

# VI

*"Something Hemingway said once about there being another dimension ..."* – Lawrence Durrell, in conversation

All roads lead to Paris, but for a writer, the burden of the effort to write in Hemingway's shadow may make it seem that all roads lead from Paris. After all, as I said to myself some years ago, Hemingway had not really written about France outside of Paris and there are many places in France that you know and love: the Camargue, for example, Aigues-Mortes, le Grau-du-Roi and Stes.-Maries-de-la-Mer and all the country around. I had written parts of a novel set there and then, in 1986, I found that Hemingway had beat me to that, too: *The Garden of Eden* was published that spring and a few weeks later I was back in the Camargue for the umpteenth time. When I visited Lawrence Durrell at his home nearby, his fabulous establishment, his maison piégeé up the road, we did not talk much about Hemingway. But halfway through the five-liter container of local wine I mentioned this problem, at least for an American, of writing about the things that Hemingway had already written about. It is, of course, a problem of both substance and style. Durrell had claimed all the numinous country of the South of France in his *Avignon Quintet* which he had just finished. Yet, marvelous, rich, and evocative as that series of novels is, the shadow cast across the landscape is not the same, at least not for an American. (For example, Durrell has written about the gypsy pilgrimage and Provençal fiesta at Stes.-Maries-de-la-Mer and I could still write about it; but what American in his right mind would write about the Pamplona fiesta after Hemingway?) When I raised the Hemingway question, Durrell did not have much to say, although he did say this: "There was something Hemingway said once about there being another dimension you could get, could break through to .... it impressed me at the time." Hemingway's commentary in *The Green Hills of Africa* about the "fifth dimension" has been much discussed with little agreement as to what he meant. Some relate it to memory, some to mysticism. I believe that Hemingway's extra dimension is compounded of memory, mystery, and love, consummated in the exhilaration and the annealment of the act of writing. It is precisely because Hemingway *did* achieve this dimension when he wrote of Paris — and a few other places — that it is very difficult for anyone to write about these places, and when we go to these places we will always go with Hemingway.

1989 is the great year of the Bicentennial in Paris. Thousands and thousands of Americans will walk the streets of Paris, many of them more aware of some version of Hemingway than any version of the Revolution. Maybe I'll go, though I don't like Paris in the summer, with all the tourists and the students with copies of *The Sun Also Rises* stuffed in their awkward backpacks. But if I go I'll take my favorite walk, around the Ile Saint Louis at night, across the bridge, pausing to look at Notre Dame, and then up the hill to the rue Saint-Jacques. Last summer when I took that walk, unconsciously following Jake and Bill in *The Sun Also Rises*, I stopped on the bridge and looked down the river at Notre Dame shaping the night sky. I overheard an American couple a few steps away, leaning on the railing, looking at the view Hemingway admired: "What's the big deal about Paris?" the man said. "Nothing here we don't have in Cleveland," the woman said. I wanted to shout, to weep, to throw them in the river, to sentence them to read Hemingway, but I said nothing. My heart silently echoed Hemingway: "It's pretty grand .... God, I love to get back."

# Afterword

In April, 1989, an editor of a rather glamorous West Coast magazine, ARETE, called me to ask if I would be interested in writing a piece on Hemingway's Paris for a special issue of the magazine that would focus on "Literary Paris." The deadline was only a few days from the time of the phone-call. At first, what with other writing deadlines looming, other plans for those next few days, it seemed an impossible assignment. Yet, responding to some deep compulsion, some prompting of the *deus loci* – that numinous susurrus of the Spirit of Place which has always whispered to me that Paris is my mystical home – on the spur of the moment I said "yes" to the telephone request. I thought about it for two days or so, confident that I knew enough about Paris, about Hemingway, to churn out something by the deadline. But it must not be, I said to myself over and over, another tired old rehash of that familiar literary terrain, another wearisome litany of the "Lost Generation" in Paris. Then, knowing that I would have to mail something the next morning, I sat down at the typewriter and wrote all night. What I ended up with at dawn was more than twice as long as what the editor had asked for. I sent it anyway, with an accompanying note saying the piece could be cut as the demands of space dictated. It was the first time I had ever given an editor carte blanche. And it is the last time I shall ever do so.

Over the next weeks and months I sweated out the appearance of the magazine. What *would* they do to my song? And, in any case, no matter what form it might take in print, was what I had so feverishly written any good? I was on the road most of that time, driving around Kentucky, Arkansas, Wyoming, Idaho, and I did not have a copy of my manuscript with me. I couldn't remember what I had written; I received no proofs, no galleys of the cut version; I had no idea what was coming. When I returned home in July the magazine came out (Volume 2, Number I; July/August 1989). There were many changes; even the title had been changed, stripped to "Hemingway's Paris," and that alone skewed the thrust of the piece. Yet before my copy arrived I received phone-calls about the essay, several from readers who knew nothing about the original manuscript: they had wonderful words of praise for the magazine version. So maybe it did work, after all; maybe the editor had made a fine job of an impossible task, discarding thousands of words from the middle of sentences and paragraphs. Then several calls came from friends who had seen the original, and they all said: "What have they *done* to your essay?"

My copies finally arrived. Every writer will at some time or another know the feeling of having lost something dearly valued, some image or phrase or paragraph hammered out in love, the veriest issue of the writer's flesh and spirit tossed into the editor's wasteheap. Yet, at first, since I had lost my original manuscript, the way the piece looked in the magazine was attractive enough, with fine illustrations and lovely typography and skillful arrangement on the page. I felt the gaps, the curious hiatuses and weakened linkage – I knew much was missing but I could not remember exactly what. Later, when the original long version did turn up in a misplaced box of miscellaneous manuscripts, I saw what my friends had meant. And I mourned the loss of what might have been decent poetry, or words, of favorite turns of phrase and a certain larger rhythm – all lost in the glamour and gloss of an expensive magazine. But why, after all, should we expect poetry in a pretty magazine? Not in the year 1989, under the reigning historical imperative: Let the People look at Pictures. Yes, instead of mere word-images there were all those clean white spaces, those elegant ample margins, the full-page photograph of Hemingway's face, the gorgeous skyline of Paris sprawling across two-pages which could have been filled with my words. A glitzy magazine is a glitzy magazine, and they pay well; I could spend several good days in Paris on the proceeds, so what did it matter?

    Finally, however, it does matter. Not long after I recovered the original manuscript, the opportunity for publication of the uncut essay presented itself. The temptation to tinker with that one-night stand, that one-sitting manuscript was strong, but I have resisted. This is it, as written that April night. The great thing about all-night letters written to those you care about deeply is the rush of feeling, the wrack and the rhythm of the attempt to name the numinous, to place the unplaceable, to speak the unspeakable and to utter what must finally be love – that love which is annealed by the fire and form of words, the storm-surf and culmination waves of sound upon sound, the spindrift of images; the kind of annealment which can only be accomplished in the singleness of night, under the dark discipline of dawn. Such letters, I reckon, should never be revised. (Whether they should be mailed is another question entirely.) Maybe this is not an essay. Maybe it is an all-night letter to Paris, to Hemingway.

>H.R. Stoneback
>Roncevaux Farm
>Gravel Switch, Kentucky

Made in the USA
Lexington, KY
31 March 2011